NORWEGIAN FJORDS CRUISE TRAVEL GUIDE 2025

Explore Breathtaking Fjords, Top Cruise Destinations, and Essential Tips for a Memorable Scandinavian Adventure

Donald M. Clark

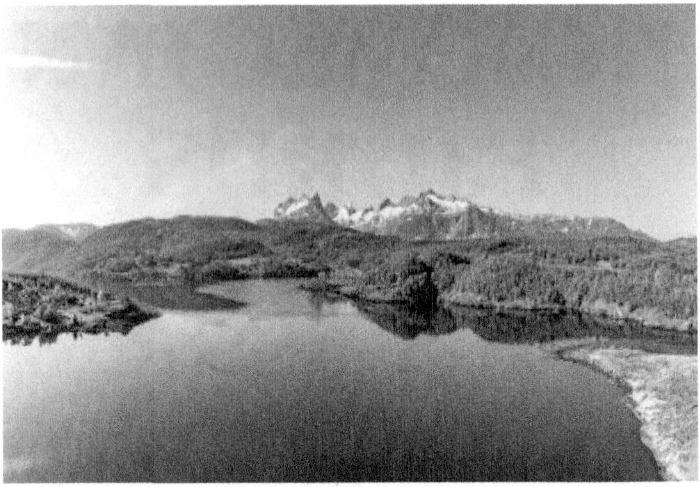

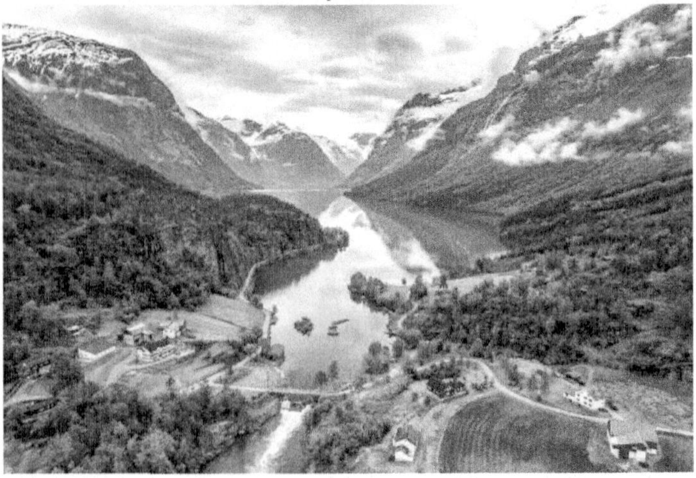

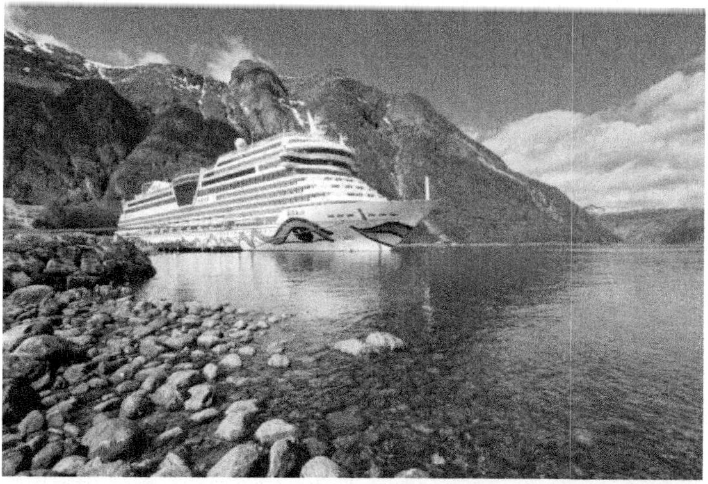

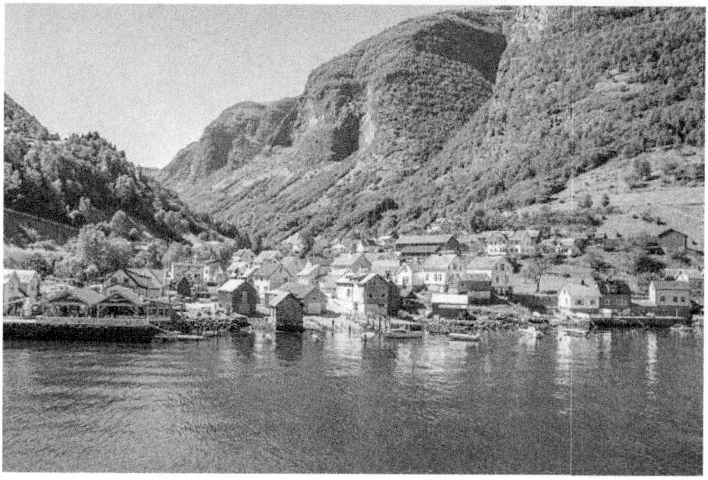

All rights reserved. No part of this publication may be reproduced, distributed, or transmitted in any form or by any means, including photocopying, recording, or other electronic or mechanical methods, without the prior written permission of the publisher, except in the case of brief quotations embodied in critical reviews and certain other noncommercial uses permitted by copyright law.

Copyright ©Donald M. Clark, 2024.

Table Of Content

MAP OF NORWEGIAN FJORDS CRUISE.................. 6
Introduction... 7
    Why Cruise the Norwegian Fjords?......................... 7
    What to Expect from This Guide?......................... 10
Chapter 1: Planning Your Norwegian Fjord Cruise. 13
    Best Time to Visit the Norwegian Fjords................. 13
    Choosing the Right Cruise Line.............................. 17
    Essential Travel Documents and Requirements..... 20
    Budget & Costs for a Fjord Cruise.......................... 23
Chapter 2: Top Cruise Routes and Destinations..... 27
    The Bergen to Kirkenes Route............................... 27
    Geirangerfjord and Alesund.................................... 32
    Sognefjord and Flam... 35
    Nordfjord and Olden.. 37
    Hardangerfjord.. 39
Chapter 3: Onboard the Cruise................................ 41
    What to Expect on a Norwegian Fjord Cruise Ship 41
    Dining and Entertainment Onboard........................ 44
    Cruise Shore Excursions.. 48
Chapter 4: Exploring the Fjords – Nature and Adventure.. 56
    Outdoor Activities in the Norwegian Fjords............ 56
    Wildlife and Natural Beauty..................................... 60
    Sustainable Travel in Fjords.................................... 63
Chapter 5: Culture and History of the Norwegian Fjords.. 66

Norwegian Folklore and Traditions.......................... 66
Historic Villages and Local Life............................... 69
Museum Visits and Cultural Hotspots..................... 71

Chapter 6: Practical Tips for Cruising the Fjords....79
Packing Tips for a Fjord Cruise................................79
Staying Connected.. 82
Health and Safety on Board and Off....................... 85

Chapter 7: Transportation in the Norwegian Fjords 89
Getting to the Norwegian Fjords............................. 89
Getting Around The Fjords...................................... 92
Cruise Ports and Shore Excursions........................ 94
Eco-Friendly Transportation.....................................98

Chapter 8: Shopping, Dining, and Souvenirs........ 101
Best Souvenirs from the Fjords............................. 101
Top Restaurants & Local Dining Experiences.......103
Shopping at Norwegian Fjord Ports...................... 108

Chapter 9: Itinerary for Norwegian Fjord Cruise....112
Day 1: Bergen.. 112
Day 2: Stavanger... 114
Day 3: Geirangerfjord.. 116
Day 4: Alesund.. 118
Day 5: Flam and Sognefjord................................. 120
Day 6: Tromsø... 122
Day 7: Return to Bergen....................................... 125

Conclusion.. 127

5

MAP OF NORWEGIAN FJORDS CRUISE

Introduction

Why Cruise the Norwegian Fjords?

Cruising through the Norwegian Fjords is an unforgettable experience that combines spectacular scenery, cultural richness, and the opportunity to immerse oneself in Norway's natural treasures. As I traveled through these magnificent fjords, I couldn't help but be captivated by the towering cliffs, gushing waterfalls, and deep, clean seas that surrounded me on all sides. Every corner I turned appeared to reveal a fresh scene, like a painting coming to life.

One of the most stunning aspects of a Norwegian fjord tour is the variety of scenery you'll see. From the world-famous Geirangerfjord, with its green seas and spectacular cliffs, to the serene beauty of Sognefjord, the country's longest and deepest fjord, the scenery is boundless and makes every experience special. Natural forces sculpt the fjords, which have been carved over millions of years by glaciers, giving them a spectacular sight to behold.

In addition to the breathtaking scenery, these voyages provide a unique look into Norwegian culture and history. Small settlements around the fjords, such as Flam and Alesund, provide insight into traditional ways of living, with the water influencing everything from cuisine to architecture. The historic timber buildings of Bryggen in Bergen, a UNESCO World Heritage site, transport you back in time to Norway's trading days, while Alesund's Art Nouveau architecture demonstrates the city's resilience following a fire in the early twentieth century.

A fjord trip also provides an opportunity to witness the Arctic's ever-changing light. Whether you're sailing beneath the Midnight Sun in the summer or following the Northern Lights in the winter, the natural light display adds an ethereal element to the experience. The peaceful tranquility of the seas and towering mountains, along with these amazing events, create an atmosphere unlike any other on Earth.

Because of their distinctive nature, these cruises appeal to a wide range of people. There's something for everyone, whether you want excitement, such as trekking up to breathtaking vistas or kayaking in the fjord's clean waters, or if you prefer to rest. Furthermore, the sophisticated ships that sail these waters offer first-rate amenities, like luxurious accommodations and world-class dining, ensuring that you enjoy both the journey and the destination.

Finally, cruising the Norwegian Fjords is more than just a journey; it's an experience that stimulates all of your senses, from the refreshing breeze on your face to the breathtaking splendor of Norway's natural landscapes. It's an opportunity to calm down, reconnect with nature, and explore a land rich in culture and natural beauty.

So, if you're asking why you should cruise the Norwegian Fjords, it's because this tour allows you to see some of the world's most beautiful scenery while also developing a strong cultural connection to the heart of Norway.

What to Expect from This Guide?

When arranging a Norwegian Fjord cruise, the sheer beauty and variety of alternatives can be overwhelming—but that's where our guide can help! Consider it your trusted companion, guiding you on an amazing journey through one of the world's most gorgeous locations. Here's how this guide can improve your planning experience:

A Roadmap for a Perfect Cruise
This book is your all-in-one reference for everything from selecting the finest fjord itineraries to comprehending what is included in your cruise package. I'll guide you through must-see places such as Geirangerfjord, Flam, and Bergen, making sure you don't miss any highlights.

This book is suitable for both first-time cruisers and seasoned travelers. I'll give you advice on how to choose the best cruise line, what's included, and how to pack. You will know exactly what to expect before you embark.

Breaking Down Each Destination
Each chapter contains up-to-date information on significant places. From what to do onshore to how to make the most of your time onboard, I've done the groundwork to make your trip stress-free. Each location includes extensive guidance to activities, cultural insights, and local cuisine.

For example, if you're fascinated about Flam, I'll explain why the Flam Railway is a must-see attraction and how to book your spot. If Bergen is on your agenda, I've included some insider suggestions for discovering Bryggen's charm and enjoying fresh seafood at the crowded Fish Market.

Customizable Tips for Any Traveler
This book offers guidance geared to your specific needs, whether you're traveling alone, with a spouse, or with your family. I've included budget tips, luxury recommendations, and kid-friendly activities to make it simple to tailor your trip. Don't worry, there's something here for everyone.

Insider Tips for a Smooth Journey
When is the greatest time of year to cruise the fjords? What is the weather like, and how should you pack? How about monetary and language tips? This resource provides solutions to these questions

and more. I've also provided transportation tips, such as traveling from the airport to the port and navigating shore excursions, so nothing is unsure.

Itineraries for Simplifying Your Planning
Sometimes the most difficult thing is deciding where to begin. That's why I've given sample itineraries, whether you're planning a fast 3-day break or a full 7-day trip. Use these itineraries as is, or modify them to suit your unique travel style.

Chapter 1: Planning Your Norwegian Fjord Cruise

Best Time to Visit the Norwegian Fjords

When organizing a trip to the Norwegian Fjords, timing is crucial. Each season has something unique to offer, whether you're looking for the Northern Lights, soaking in the Midnight Sun, or admiring waterfalls at their peak. Based on the most recent research, here's a month-by-month guide to deciding when the best time to visit the fjords is.

Spring (March – May)

Spring is a season for regeneration in the Norwegian Fjords. Snow begins to melt, causing the waterfalls to reach their most majestic levels. By May, temperatures range from 5°C to 15°C (41°F to 59°F), and the days become longer, allowing you to explore more.

Highlights

March: Late winter lingers, making it ideal for skiing or viewing the Northern Lights in northern locations.

April-May: Fruit trees bloom in fjordside settlements such as Hardangerfjord, and hiking routes are less crowded.

Activities include early-season hiking, beautiful drives, and fjord cruises that offer breathtaking views of roaring waterfalls.

Summer (June-August)
Summer is peak season in the fjords, with temperatures ranging from 10°C to 25°C (50°F to 77°F) and extended daylight hours thanks to the Midnight Sun. This is the optimal time for outdoor activities and boating calm waters.

Highlights

June: Waterfalls remain forceful, and the Midnight Sun rises in the north.

July-August: The warm weather is great for kayaking, hiking, and exploring communities. Expect beautiful, green scenery.

Activity

- Hiking notable hikes such as Pulpit Rock (Preikestolen) and Trolltunga.

- Kayak through calm fjords.

- Attending local festivals, such as Bergenfest.

Pro Tip: Summer is the busiest season, so book cruises and accommodations well in advance.

Autumn (September–November)

Autumn delivers gorgeous foliage and quieter fjords as the people think. Temperatures drop to 2°C to 15°C (36°F to 59°F), particularly in late October.

Highlights

- September is ideal for late-season hiking in beautiful scenery.

- From October to November, Northern Lights sightings become increasingly common as darkness returns.

- Activities include harvest festivals and fruit picking in locations such as Hardangerfjord.

- Photography aficionados will appreciate the gorgeous fall colors and tranquil waters.

Winter (December - February)
Winter turns the fjords into a beautiful wonderland. While fjord cruises are available year-round, fewer run in the north. In most locations, temperatures fluctuate between -6°C and 3°C (21°F to 37°F).

Highlights

- Snow Capped summits and ice waterfalls.

- Experience Northern Lights tours in Tromsø or near the Arctic Circle.

- Activities include dog sledding, skiing and snowshoeing.

- Relaxing evenings in traditional Norwegian cabins or on cruises.

Pro Tip: Winter is the best time to visit for a quieter, more mystical ambiance at a reduced cost.

Month-by-month Recommendations

- Peak waterfall season is from May to early June (melting snow creates spectacular waterfalls).

- The best months for hiking are July through early September (warm weather and clear paths).

- The best months for seeing the Northern Lights are November through February (length evenings and clear skies).

- The best months for avoiding crowds are April, September, and October.

Choosing the Right Cruise Line

When arranging a Norwegian fjord cruise, selecting the right cruise line is one of the most important stages in ensuring an unforgettable experience. With so many possibilities, I've spent some time researching the most popular cruise lines—Hurtigruten, Viking, and MSC Cruises—and what they have to offer. Here is what I have learned:

Hurtigruten

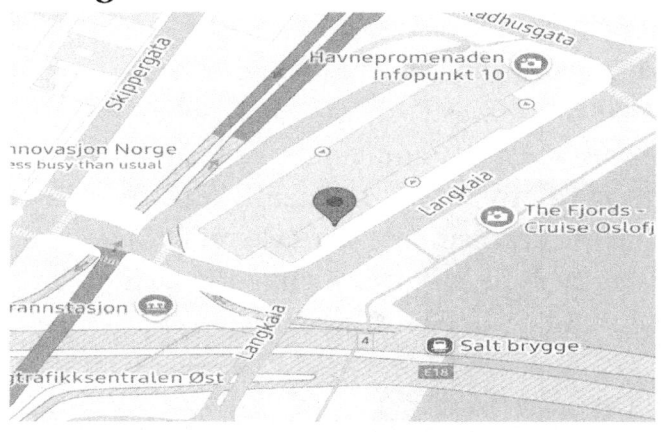

If you're looking for an authentic, local experience, Hurtigruten stands out. This line, dubbed "The World's Most Beautiful Voyage," focuses on coastal Norway. Their smaller ships can reach remote fjords and settlements that larger vessels cannot. Hurtigruten cruises also emphasize the region's culture and nature. They include activities such as hiking, kayaking, and talks on Norwegian history and wildlife. Their expedition cruises are ideal for adventurous tourists or those interested in sustainable travel, as the company is committed to environmentally responsible operations.

Viking Cruises

Viking is associated with both luxury and cultural immersion. Their programs focus on tailored beach excursions and onboard enrichment. Viking's ships are intended for comfort, with large accommodations and a tranquil, Scandinavian-inspired aesthetic. What really appealed to me was their "no kids" policy, which is ideal for a calm, adults-only encounter. Their Norwegian fjord cruises frequently feature visits to prominent destinations like Geirangerfjord and Flam, as well as cultural highlights such as local cooking courses or historical tours.

MSC Cruises

MSC Cruises offers a more family-friendly option by combining price and outstanding amenities. Their ships are huge and modern, with activities for all ages including pools, spas, and kids' clubs. While they may not have the same small-ship intimacy as Hurtigruten or the boutique feel of Viking, they do provide an excellent balance of pricing and quality. MSC's fjord cruises often focus on the main sites, such as Stavanger and Bergen, making them an excellent choice for first-time visitors to Norway.

What Cruise Line Is Best for You?

When Deciding, Examine your Priorities

- **Adventure and culture:** Hurtigruten provides deep, real exploration.

- **Luxury and relaxation:** Viking combines elegance with cultural richness.

- **Family-friendly and budget-friendly:** MSC offers a comprehensive experience for groups of all sizes.

Essential Travel Documents and Requirements

When arranging a Norwegian Fjord cruise, be sure you have the necessary travel documents and meet foreign travel regulations to ensure a smooth experience. Here's a personal guide based on the most recent developments to assist you overcome immigration, health, and safety issues.

Visa Requirements

For many travelers, entering Norway and the Schengen Zone requires advance planning:

EU/EEA Citizens
If you are from an EU/EEA nation, you will not require a visa to visit Norway. Just make sure you have a valid passport or national ID card.

Non-EU/EEA Travelers
Travelers from the United States, Canada, Australia, and the United Kingdom can travel without a visa for up to 90 days within a 180-day period. Your passport must be valid for at least three months after your scheduled departure date.

Schengen Visa
If you are from a nation that requires a visa to enter the Schengen Zone, apply for a short-term visa (type C) in advance. Make sure you have proof of lodging, travel insurance, and a return ticket.

ETIAS Requirement
Beginning in 2025, passengers from visa-exempt nations must obtain an ETIAS permit before visiting Schengen countries, including Norway.

Health Considerations
Staying knowledgeable about health regulations is critical, especially in today's travel world.

Vaccines
While Norway does not require any special vaccines for admission, it is recommended that you stay current on normal immunizations such as tetanus and measles.

COVID-19 Updates
Although most COVID-related entry restrictions have been abolished, some cruise companies may still request proof of immunization or a negative test prior to boarding. Always check your cruise operator's unique restrictions.

Travel Insurance
You must have comprehensive insurance. It should include medical crises, evacuations, and trip cancellations. Healthcare in Norway is great, yet it can be expensive without insurance.

Safety Considerations
Norway is one of the safest countries in the world, but it's always good to be prepared:

Weather Awareness
The weather in Norway's fjords can be unpredictable. Pack layered clothing and waterproof gear for your outings.

Local Laws
Follow local norms, such as the Allemannsretten (Right to Roam), which grants the public access to nature but requires duty to protect it.

Emergency Contacts
Keep important numbers like 112 and the nearest consulate or embassy.

Budget & Costs for a Fjord Cruise

When planning for a Fjord Cruise, it's critical to examine a variety of elements that will affect the entire cost, including cruise packages and additional onshore activities. Here's a breakdown based on recent revisions to help you prepare efficiently.

Cost Estimates for a Fjord Cruise
The cost of a Norwegian Fjord Cruise varies according to the cruise line, duration, and level of luxury. A three-day trip normally costs between $500 and $1,000 USD per person for a standard stateroom. A 7-day cruise might cost between $1,000 and $2,500 USD per person, depending on the amenities and cruise line you choose.

Luxury cruises or more exclusive packages, such as those including shore excursions, premium cuisine, and suite-level lodgings, can easily cost more than $5,000 USD per person for a seven-day itinerary. These cruises frequently provide improved experiences, such as private tours, premium meals, and specialist excursions like Northern Lights hunting or whale viewing.

Cruise Packages
Most cruise lines provide a variety of packages to suit different budgets. Here are some instances.

Standard Packages
These are the most basic and affordable alternatives, which usually include your stateroom, meals, and access to onboard amenities.

All-inclusive Packages
These packages feature additional benefits like shore excursions, luxury dining selections, drinks, and Wi-Fi. While these packages can be more expensive, they frequently provide greater value for individuals looking to make the most of their cruise experience.

Family or Group Discounts

Many cruise lines provide discounts to families or parties vacationing together. These discounts can considerably reduce per-person costs, particularly for bigger groups.

Off-Peak Discounts
Traveling during the off season (usually in the fall and spring) can also help you save money. This is when cruise lines give large discounts since demand is low.

How to Save on Your Fjord Cruise
Here are a few strategies for keeping costs down while enjoying a stunning fjord cruise:

Book Early
Early bookings may include lower rates or special promotions, such as free upgrades or shore excursions.

Consider Interior Cabins
While outdoor accommodations with balconies provide spectacular views, they are typically more expensive. Opting for an inside cabin can save you a lot of money without sacrificing your entire experience.

Plan your Shore Excursions Wisely

While many cruise lines provide shore excursions, they can rapidly add up. You can save money by researching ports alone. Cities such as Bergen and Alesund are easier to travel on your own, and local tours are significantly less expensive than those offered by cruise lines.

Look for Deals and Promotions
Keep an eye out for seasonal discounts, last-minute specials, and limited-time promos. Cruise lines frequently offer attractive discounts, particularly during the off-season.

Limit Extras Onboard
Wi-Fi, luxury cuisine, and spa services are frequently chargeable extras on cruise ships. To keep prices down, use the ship's basic services and avoid spending money on extras unless they are included in your package.

Chapter 2: Top Cruise Routes and Destinations

The Bergen to Kirkenes Route

Traveling the Bergen to Kirkenes route, one of Norway's most famous treks down the coast, will provide you with an unforgettable experience. This itinerary, also known as the Hurtigruten Coastal Voyage, takes you on an incredible journey across Norway's fjords, islands, and Arctic nature.

Highlights and Notable Stops

Tromsø

Tromsø, sometimes known as the "Gateway to the Arctic," is a well-known station along the route. The city is located in the Arctic Circle and offers a distinct blend of culture, history, and natural beauty. You can go to Polaria, an Arctic wildlife museum, or see the breathtaking Arctic Cathedral. Tromsø is a prime location for viewing the Northern Lights throughout winter.

Lofoten Islands

The Lofoten Islands are one of the most spectacular places you'll visit. These islands are known for their stunning landscapes, which include towering peaks, deep fjords, and attractive fishing communities. If you enjoy photography, hiking, or simply taking in the natural splendor, the Lofoten Islands are a must-see. You can visit Reine, a village generally regarded as one of the most beautiful in the world, and soak up the charm of its quaint streets and environs.

Alta

Alta, located in far northern Norway, is frequently included as a stop on the journey, serving as a gateway to Arctic activities. The Alta Museum explains ancient rock engravings that are UNESCO-listed, and the town itself is a terrific place to experience Arctic life.

Kirkenes

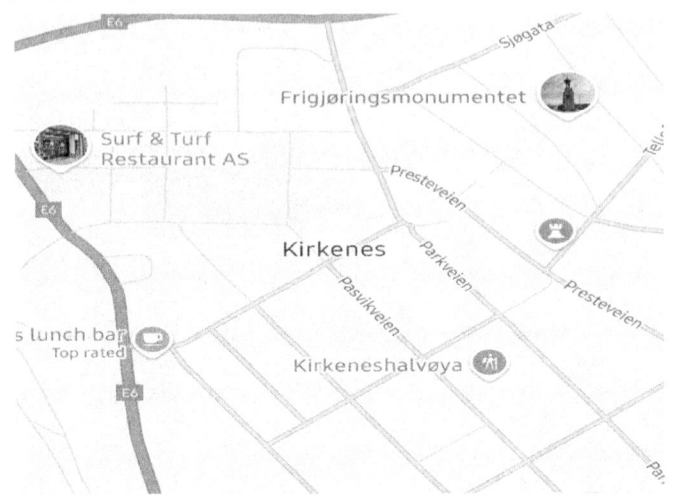

The voyage concludes in Kirkenes, a hamlet on the Russian border where you may see civilization's final outpost before venturing into the Arctic wilderness. Kirkenes has one-of-a-kind attractions, such as the Snowhotel, which is totally formed of snow and ice and provides an excellent opportunity to learn about the region's history and culture.

This route provides more than simply a gorgeous drive; it immerses you in Norway's spectacular scenery and northern culture, making it an unforgettable experience. Whether you're here to tour the lovely islands or to see the Northern Lights, you'll remember this vacation for a long time.

Geirangerfjord and Alesund

When I visited Geirangerfjord and Alesund, I was completely enthralled by the breathtaking scenery and many experiences that these places had to offer. Here's a sneak glimpse at what you shouldn't miss while touring these amazing places in Norway.

Geirangerfjord

The Geirangerfjord is widely regarded as one of the most stunning fjords in the world, and I can attest that it lives up to its reputation. As I cruised across the fjord, I was surrounded by towering cliffs and stunning waterfalls, including the famed Seven Sisters Waterfall. The way the waterfalls cascade down the steep mountainsides is mesmerizing—each of the seven streams has a distinct, graceful flow that I couldn't take my eyes away from.

One of the finest ways to properly appreciate the fjord is to go up to Dalsnibba, which has one of the best panoramic views of Geirangerfjord. From this vantage point, I could see the fjord's intricate, twisting patterns, framed by lush green slopes and majestic peaks. The trek there via the Geiranger Skywalk was a highlight for me; it's a must-do if you want to see one of Norway's best sights.

If you're feeling daring, I recommend taking a kayak excursion around the fjord, where you may paddle in tranquil waters surrounded by rocks. Of course, taking a boat tour down the fjord is a terrific opportunity to get up close to the waterfalls and towering rock walls, making it an unforgettable element of any Geiranger visit.

Alesund

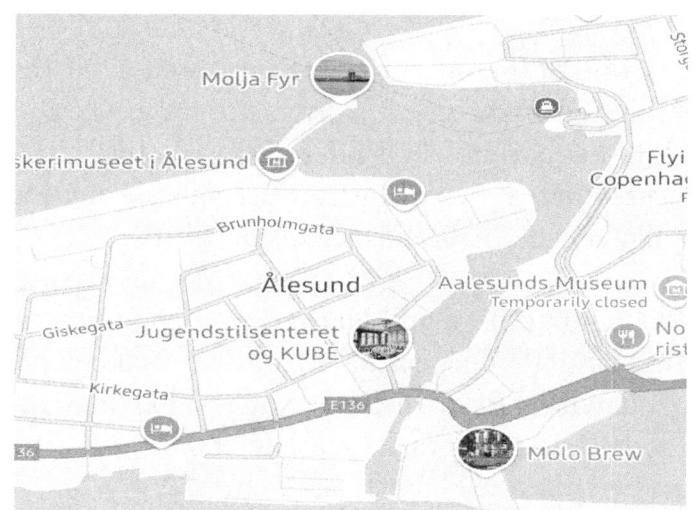

Next, I traveled to Alesund, a delightful town with a particular Art Nouveau architectural style. The town is small but full of character, and walking around the streets seemed like I was entering into a fantasy. The Art Nouveau Centre delves deeper into Alesund's history and architecture, highlighting how the town was rebuilt following a disastrous fire in 1904.

Alesund's Aksla Viewpoint was another memorable stop. After a brief trek up the hill, I was rewarded with panoramic views of the town, its surrounding islands, and the magnificent fjords in the distance. The view of the Atlantic Ocean and Sunnmøre Alps is breathtaking, especially when the light shines off the water at sunset.

For a one-of-a-kind experience, I also visited the Atlantic Sea Park, one of Northern Europe's largest saltwater aquariums. It is not only instructive, but it also provides a view into the surrounding marine life, like playful seals and schools of fish.

Both Geirangerfjord and Alesund are rich in natural beauty and unique cultural features, making my trip memorable. Whether you're looking for outdoor adventures or to soak up the local charm, these two places will not disappoint.

Sognefjord and Flam

When visiting the Sognefjord and Flam, you will have a wonderful experience. As I traveled through the Sognefjord, I was struck by its pure beauty. It is known as Norway's longest and deepest fjord, stretching 200 kilometers (124 miles) and reaching depths of more than 1,300 meters (4,265 ft). The fjord is flanked by high cliffs, lush green valleys, and gushing waterfalls, resulting in a breathtaking landscape.

Flam, a little community tucked at the innermost tip of the Sognefjord, is also lovely. I strolled through its lovely streets, which were lined with colorful mansions on the hillsides. What struck me the most was the tranquillity of the location, where the speed of life is much slower, providing the ideal retreat from the rush and bustle.

A trip to Flam is incomplete without experiencing the Flam Railway, one of the most picturesque rail journeys in the world. As the train worked its way through the steep mountainside, I was treated to stunning views of waterfalls, deep ravines, and verdant forests. The voyage was both exhilarating and calm, providing an up-close view of Norway's natural splendor.

For those looking to explore further, a boat tour on Sognefjord offers a breathtaking view of the fjord from the water, allowing you to see the spectacular cliffs and lovely settlements that line its banks. There is also the option of trekking in the adjacent mountains or visiting sights such as Flam's Viking Village or the Stegastein Viewpoint, which offers panoramic views of the fjord below.

Whether you're relaxing by the ocean in Flam or taking a thrilling journey into the mountains on the

Flam Railway, the combination of natural treasures and tranquil communities makes Sognefjord and Flam a must-see for any Norwegian adventure.

Nordfjord and Olden

When I visited Nordfjord and Olden, I was astounded by their serene, pristine beauty. These fjords are less congested than more popular destinations such as Geirangerfjord or Sognefjord, making them excellent for those seeking peace and spectacular natural scenery.

Nordfjord is recognized for its breathtaking beauty, including high mountains, glaciers, and charming settlements. One of my favorite experiences was hiking along the Briksdalsbreen Glacier in Olden. The hike was quite straightforward, but it provided stunning views of the ice-blue glacier and the surrounding valley. The road leads you through lush forests, across streams, and over little bridges, providing a calm and immersive experience. For a more demanding trek, consider Mount Skåla, the highest peak in the Nordfjord region, which provides panoramic views of the fjord and surrounding area.

Olden's village charm is evident. It's tucked away at the edge of the Oldenfjord, and exploring it on foot or by bike is a relaxing experience. There are numerous hiking paths, ranging from moderate stroll to hard climbs. I recommend the Olden Valley hike, which leads through a lovely valley surrounded by mountains. The peacefulness here, with only the sounds of birds and moving rivers, was like walking into another universe.

What I liked about these regions was the opportunity to connect with nature in a way that felt close and personal. They're ideal for people wishing to get away from the crowds of more touristy areas while still experiencing Norway's magnificent fjord landscapes. If you prefer trekking and exploring rural areas, Nordfjord and Olden are must-see destinations.

For additional information on these fjord regions and their hiking paths, visit the Official Norway Travel website and Visit Norway's hiking guides, which provide thorough recommendations and directions.

Hardangerfjord

When I visited Hardangerfjord, I was charmed by its natural splendor, which is often regarded as one of Norway's most attractive fjords. Hardangerfjord, known for its stunning waterfalls and vivid fruit orchards, provides a tranquil getaway into nature, with lush green landscapes that contrast nicely with steep cliffs and sparkling seas.

The region's highlight is the famed Vøringsfossen waterfall, which cascades down 182 meters. The view is stunning, especially in the spring and early summer, when the snow melts and the water runs rapidly. Along with the waterfalls, the fjord is bordered by an abundance of orchards that produce the region's famous apples, pears, and cherries. Visiting during the harvest season provides an excellent opportunity to try local fruits and savor their crisp, fresh flavors.

Hardangerfjord also has a rich local culture. The little communities that line the fjord's beaches, such as Ulvik and Norheimsund, provide a flavor of traditional Norwegian living, complete with comfortable wooden houses and lively local festivals. These settlements celebrate their heritage, offering opportunities to enjoy old Norse traditions, local cuisine, and specialty crafts.

Whether you want to explore the outdoors or immerse yourself in the peaceful culture of the fjord, Hardangerfjord has something for everyone. It's an ideal place for anyone looking for both adventure and relaxation in one of Norway's most scenic areas.

Chapter 3: Onboard the Cruise

What to Expect on a Norwegian Fjord Cruise Ship

When you board a Norwegian fjord cruise ship, you enter a floating refuge designed to provide luxury, leisure, and adventure. Here's what to expect in terms of onboard facilities and services based on current cruise travel patterns.

Luxurious Amenities
Modern Norwegian fjord cruise ships are designed with your comfort in mind. Expect spacious cabins, many with individual balconies that provide

panoramic views of the fjords. Suites frequently have additional amenities such as priority boarding, complimentary dining upgrades, and private lounge access. If you're traveling alone, some cruise lines provide comfortable single-occupancy accommodations.

World-Class Dining
The food options on board are nothing short of outstanding. From fine-dining restaurants serving locally inspired meals (such as salmon, cod, or reindeer) to informal buffets and poolside grills, there's something for everyone's taste. Many ships also have specialized restaurants serving cuisines such as Italian, Asian fusion, and steakhouse classics. Don't pass on the afternoon tea service or late-night snack bars for in-between desires.

Entertainment and Activities
While the fjords are the highlight of the show, onboard entertainment keeps you entertained throughout your cruise. Theaters showcase a variety of live acts, including musicals and comedy shows. Some cruises also include guest lectures on Norwegian culture, history, or nature, which are ideal for complementing your experience.

Active visitors can find exercise centers with sophisticated equipment, yoga courses, and even rock-climbing walls or basketball fields. If you prefer relaxation, spas provide massages, facials, and thermal suites to revitalize your senses.

Kid-Friendly Features
Traveling with family? Norwegian fjord cruise ships are often family-friendly, with separate facilities for kids and teens. Look for water slides, children's clubs with supervised activities, and even mini-golf courses. Meanwhile, parents may relax knowing that their children are entertained.

Exceptional Services
Onboard service is excellent, with workers going above and beyond to ensure a seamless journey. You'll feel taken care of, from concierge services that assist you schedule shore excursions to 24-hour room service for late-night desires. Some cruise lines even provide specialized butler services to suit passengers.

Unique Features for Fjord Cruises
Many ships are built to enhance the fjord cruise experience. Expect spacious viewing platforms with floor-to-ceiling glass that provide uninterrupted views of towering cliffs and tumbling waterfalls.

Some cruise lines also offer themed nights, such as Nordic cuisine tastings or storytelling sessions inspired by Viking mythology.

Sustainability

Many Norwegian fjord cruises are making efforts toward sustainability. To protect the pristine beauty of the fjords, ships are equipped with hybrid engines or emissions-reducing technologies, in accordance with Norwegian environmental standards.

Onboard, life is a mix of luxury and adventure. Whether you're relaxing in the hot tub while watching the fjords pass by or learning about Norwegian history from an onboard expert, every moment feels carefully planned for a wonderful experience.

Dining and Entertainment Onboard

Dining and entertainment on a Norwegian Fjord cruise offer an ideal balance of cultural immersion and relaxation. As you sail through the fjords, you'll have plenty of opportunities to indulge in Norwegian food, as well as a choice of entertainment alternatives that highlight the country's cultural traditions.

Norwegian Cuisine

Norwegian cuisine is heavily anchored in the country's natural resources, emphasizing fresh, locally sourced foods. Menus onboard are likely to include typical Norwegian cuisine that emphasize the country's rich culinary heritage. Seafood is very important, especially dishes like fresh salmon, king crab, and cod, which are classics in Norwegian cuisine. Rømmegrøt, a creamy sour cream porridge, is a popular comfort food, commonly served with cured meats and sugar. For those with a sweet craving, koldtbord, a Scandinavian-style smorgasbord with cured meats, cheeses, and bread, is not to be missed.

Additionally, most ships provide buffet-style meals with a variety of Norwegian and foreign alternatives. There are both heavy and lighter options, such as salads, smoked fish, and Norwegian flatbreads. In the evening, expect multi-course dinners with a more formal feel, generally featuring a combination of traditional Norwegian foods and international cuisine.

Many cruise lines also include specialty dining options, where you may taste more refined Norwegian fare, such as a traditional Norwegian supper, which generally includes delicacies like raspeballer (potato dumplings) or perfectly cooked lamb shanks.

Onboard Cultural Entertainment
Cruising through the breathtaking fjord vistas is an unforgettable experience, but the onboard cultural entertainment takes it to the next level. Many Norwegian fjord cruises feature live performances and cultural events that highlight Norway's diverse traditions. You might appreciate performances of Norwegian folk music, which frequently includes traditional instruments like the Hardanger fiddle, as well as dances inspired by the Norwegian countryside.

Expect themed evenings that will immerse you in Norwegian culture. For example, there may be a Viking night, in which the ship organizes events and entertainment inspired by Norway's Viking heritage. These evenings frequently feature costumes, storytelling, and dance performances that bring Norway's history and mythology to life in an exciting way.

Furthermore, many ships have Nordic-inspired lounges where you can relax while listening to music that matches the country's natural

46

beauty—imagine listening to peaceful Nordic jazz or energetic Scandinavian pop while sailing past snow-capped mountains and crystal-clear waterways.

Whether you're eating on fresh seafood or watching a live performance inspired by Norwegian traditions, the food and entertainment on a Norwegian Fjord cruise are a lovely opportunity to immerse yourself in Norway's culture and natural beauty.

Cruise Shore Excursions

When it comes to cruise shore excursions in the Norwegian Fjords, the selections are stunning and diverse, with something for everyone. Based on current information, here are my personal recommendations for day trips and tours in some of the most popular sites you're likely to visit on a Norwegian Fjord cruise:

Bergen

Recommended Excursions

Mount Fløyen and Funicular Tour

Begin the day by taking the Fløibanen Funicular up Mount Fløyen for panoramic views of Bergen and its neighboring fjords. From there, you can take a short trek through peaceful forest paths.

Bryggen Walking Tour
A guided walking tour of the UNESCO-designated Bryggen area is essential. While strolling through these bright wooden houses, I was transported back to Bergen's Hanseatic trading days.

Hardangerfjord Day Trip
For those with extra time, take a day excursion to the Hardangerfjord region, where you can see spectacular waterfalls like Steinsdalsfossen and orchards full of delicious apples in season.

Geiranger

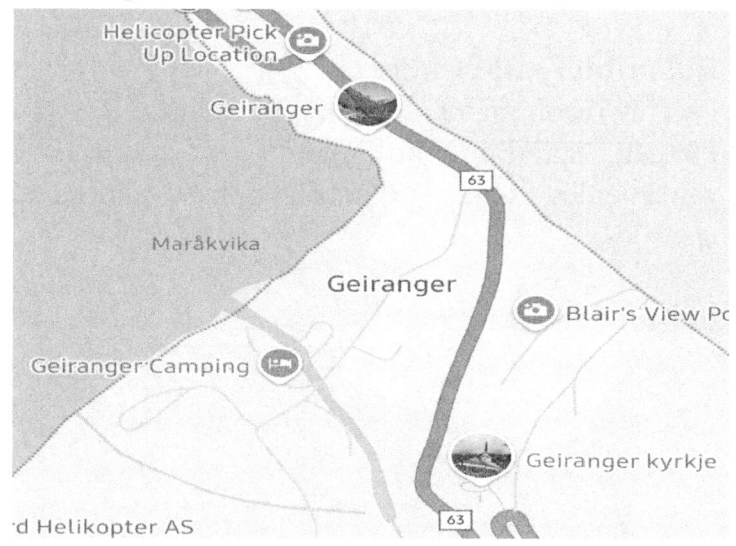

Recommended Excursions

Seven Sisters Waterfall Cruise
One of the highlights is a closer look at the famous Seven Sisters Waterfall. A boat trip allows you to float right up to the waterfalls while learning about the fjord's history.

Eagle Road (Ørnevegen Drive)
For thrill enthusiasts, a tour along Eagle Road provides hairpin curves and breathtaking vistas of

the fjord below. Don't miss the Eagle's Bend Viewpoint for an ideal photo opportunity.

Dalsnibba's Skywalk
I highly recommend seeing the Dalsnibba Mountain Plateau. Standing 1,500 meters above sea level, you'll enjoy some of Norway's best panoramic vistas.

Flam

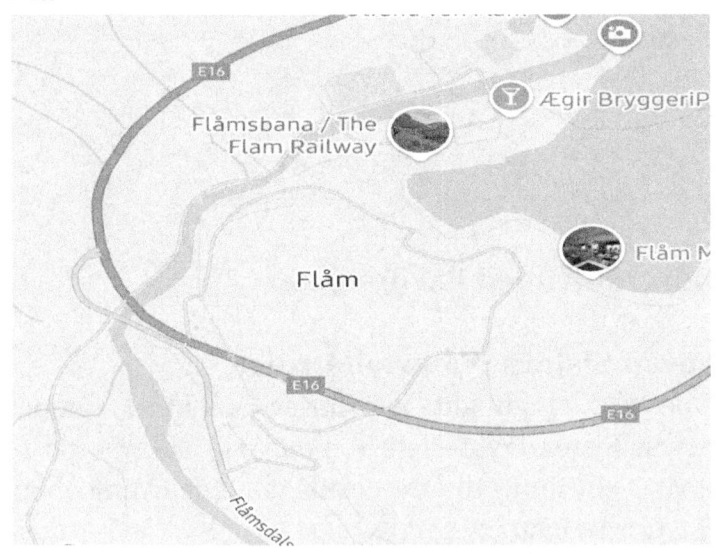

Recommended Excursions

Flam's Railway Journey

This gorgeous train ride is a must! As I traveled by train, I marveled at the steep mountains, waterfalls, and beautiful villages. It's a popular attraction among visitors.

Naerøyfjord Cruise
A short trip through Nærøyfjord, a UNESCO World Heritage site, highlights narrow fjord channels surrounded by towering rocks.

Stegastein's Viewpoint
A guided trip to this new overlook provides amazing views of the fjord and landscapes. It's a tranquil area to take in the beauty of nature.

Alesund

Recommended Excursions

Art Nouveau Walking Tour
Alesund's architecture is unique to Norway. During this guided tour, I saw its bright Art Nouveau structures and learned about how the city was rebuilt following a devastating fire in 1904.

Aksla Viewpoint and Fjellstua Hike
I recommend trekking up to Aksla Viewpoint or taking the bus. The view of Alesund and the neighboring islands is well worth it.

Hjørundfjord Day Cruise
Hjørundfjord, less busy than Geirangerfjord, offers serene waters and breathtaking scenery. It's a hidden gem for anyone looking for a quieter fjord experience.

Tromsø

Recommended Excursions

Arctic Cathedral and Cable Car
Visit the renowned Arctic Cathedral before riding the Fjellheisen Cable Car to Mount Storsteinen for panoramic views of the Arctic countryside.

Whale Watching (seasonal)
Whale-watching cruises, depending on when you visit, can be unforgettable. Seeing these amazing creatures in their natural environment was humbling for me.

Northern Lights Chase (Winter)
If your trip is during the winter, plan a guided tour to see the spectacular Northern Lights.

These trips provide a variety of cultural, historical, and environmental attractions that appeal to a wide range of interests. Whether you like peaceful sightseeing or strenuous treks, these tours will enhance your Norwegian Fjord cruise experience.

Chapter 4: Exploring the Fjords – Nature and Adventure

Outdoor Activities in the Norwegian Fjords

When it comes to outdoor activities in the Norwegian Fjords, I was completely intrigued by the variety of adventures available to all types of travelers. Whether you want a physical challenge or a peaceful getaway into nature, the fjords offer a playground for outdoor enthusiasts. Here are some activities that had a lasting impact:

Hiking through Breathtaking Landscapes

The trekking opportunities in the fjords are fantastic. One of my personal favorites is the hike up Preikestolen (Pulpit Rock) near Lysefjord. The vista from the top, with a precipitous drop of nearly 600 meters to the lake below, is stunning. Another must-hike is the trek to Trolltunga (Troll's Tongue), which provides a unique photo opportunity with its distinctive rock jutting out over the fjord.

For something less challenging, the Aurlandsdalen Valley has a variety of moderate paths that run through gorgeous valleys, cascading rivers, and tranquil lakes. The trails are well-marked and cater to various skill levels, making them ideal for both families and single travelers.

Kayaking in the Still Water

Kayaking provided me with a unique viewpoint on the fjords. Gliding along the peaceful, mirror-like waters of Geirangerfjord or Naerøyfjord gave me an incredible sensation of peace. I was able to paddle close to tumbling waterfalls like the Seven Sisters and pass beneath towering cliffs, enjoying the overwhelming size of the fjords in a way that is impossible to do from a cruise ship's deck.

Guided kayak outings are widely offered and ideal for beginners. They frequently contain unique insights about the region's history and geology, which enhances the experience.

Immersive Nature Walks
For those who prefer a slower pace, nature excursions in the Norwegian Fjords are a treat. One of my most memorable walks was through Flam, where walkways wind along the shore of the Sognefjord, providing constant photo opportunities. Wildflowers bloom in bright colors throughout the spring and summer, and sheep can often be seen grazing in the meadows.

I also explored Romsdalseggen Ridge, which combines moderate walking trails with panoramic views. These hikes are ideal for taking in the splendor of the fjords without the exertion of a longer journey.

Pro Tips for Outdoor Adventures

Dress in layers: Bring a rain jacket as the weather in the fjords can change quickly.

Footwear: Hiking boots are required for rough trails, although sturdy sneakers are sufficient for kayaking or simple hikes.

Guides and Tours: If you're new to the area, local guides may help you get the most out of it by pointing out hidden jewels and providing safety recommendations.

Outdoor activities in the Norwegian Fjords are more than just adventures; they provide an opportunity to connect directly with nature. From exhilarating treks to peaceful paddling sessions, every encounter here feels like a story worth telling. Whether you're an ardent adventurer or simply want to immerse yourself in Norway's natural beauty, there are plenty of opportunities to create amazing moments in the fjords.

Wildlife and Natural Beauty

Going on a trek across the Norwegian Fjords was like entering a real-life nature documentary. The region's natural splendor is unrivaled, and the profusion of wildlife gives a wonderful touch to every moment. As I cruised through these legendary fjords, I came across numerous possibilities to photograph gorgeous animals in their natural habitats.

Animal Sightings
The fjords are rich with species, both on land and underwater. I was lucky enough to observe pods of playful porpoises surfing the ship's wake, as well as humpback whales breaching in the distance—a photographer's dream! Along the rocky shorelines, I

60

kept an eye out for seals soaking in the sun. Bird fans will be delighted, since the fjords are a home for seabirds like puffins and white-tailed eagles, which may be seen flying magnificently over the cliffs.

During a guided excursion in Tromsø, visitors witnessed tranquil reindeer grazing in the cold landscapes. It felt like a scene from a winter postcard. If you travel during the right season, you might be able to see the elusive Arctic fox or musk oxen in the northern regions.

Scenic Photography Tips
Capturing the sense of this pristine wilderness was one of the trip's pleasures. Here are a few strategies that helped me get postcard-worthy shots:

Golden Hours: The greatest lighting occurs at sunrise and sunset, when the fjords are drenched in golden light. These hours make the ocean, rocks, and sky appear truly magnificent.

Zoom in on Wildlife: A zoom lens is essential when photographing birds or marine life. Patience is essential—waiting for the ideal moment, such as a puffin in flight or a whale's tail flipping above the water, is well worthwhile.

Wide Angles for Landscapes: A wide-angle lens can help you capture the grandeur of the fjords. It emphasizes the size of the cliffs and the depth of the canals, making your photographs as breathtaking as the real thing.

Stability is Essential: Whether on a moving cruise or a smaller excursion boat, a tripod or stabilizer for your camera ensures excellent shots regardless of movement.

Weather and Reflections: Overcast days can provide dramatic skies that reflect brilliantly on the lake, so don't avoid them.

Why is it Worth Exploring?
Beyond photography, merely witnessing these animals in such clean settings felt like a deeper connection to nature. Whether you're a serious animal enthusiast or a casual nature lover, the Norwegian Fjords offer an unrivaled opportunity to appreciate Earth's natural splendor.

With each magnificent scenery and wildlife interaction, I was left with not only images but also memories that will last a lifetime. If you're planning a trip, remember to carry binoculars, a high-quality camera, and, most importantly, a feeling of wonder—you never know what magnificent sight awaits you just around the corner.

Sustainable Travel in Fjords

When I visited the Norwegian Fjords, I recognized that maintaining their natural beauty is critical for future generations. Sustainable tourism is no longer just a trend; it is a necessity, particularly in endangered environments like these. Here are some practical techniques I learned to lessen my environmental impact while seeing these breathtaking settings.

Choose Eco-friendly Cruises
The first step in achieving sustainable fjord cruising is to choose an environmentally conscious cruise line. Many cruise firms in Norway now use hybrid or electric-powered ships to reduce carbon emissions. For example, any cruises into the Geirangerfjord must now fulfill strict zero-emission criteria, making this location one of the world's most environmentally sensitive cruise areas. When reserving, I sought for certificates such as "Green Tourism" and "Eco-Lighthouse."

Pack Light and Smart

Packing light reduces the ship's weight, which might result in decreased fuel usage. I packed reusable goods like water bottles, shopping bags, and travel utensils. This not only reduced my consumption of single-use plastics, but it also increased my awareness of my total impact.

Support Local and Sustainable Businesses
Every stop along the fjords provides wonderful possibilities to interact with local populations. I chose excursions offered by small, environmentally friendly businesses, such as guided nature walks or kayaking tours led by locals. Supporting these enterprises immediately supports the region's economy while not burdening the environment.

Respect Nature
One of the most pleasant aspects of my fjord tour was trekking the paths near Flam and Geiranger. While exploring, I adhered to Leave No Trace guidelines, sticking on designated routes and avoiding upsetting wildlife. I even participated in a group cleanup campaign in Flam, which was a wonderful and rewarding opportunity to give back.

Reduce Energy Consumption Onboard
Even minor actions on the ship can make an impact. When I left my cabin, I always shut off the

lights and electronics to avoid wasting water. Some cruise lines also offer recycling initiatives onboard, and I made an effort to join.

Learn and Advocate

The most striking aspect of my vacation was how much I learnt about the fjords' delicate ecosystems. Many cruise companies now offer educational seminars on sustainability, which helped me better comprehend the influence of tourism on these settings. Armed with this information, I make it a point to promote sustainable travel practices whenever I share my experiences.

Chapter 5: Culture and History of the Norwegian Fjords

Norwegian Folklore and Traditions

When I first started researching Norwegian folklore and traditions, I was struck by the breadth of the stories and practices that have defined this lovely country's identity. Norway's past, which includes old legends of mythological creatures as well as deeply embedded cultural customs, provides insight into its people's relationship with environment and history.

Mythical Stories and Legends

Troll stories are among the most captivating features of Norwegian mythology. These tall, often terrifying animals are thought to live in the mountains and woodlands, protecting treasures or causing problems for travelers. As I toured the fjords, it was clear how the dramatic settings could inspire such stories—steep cliffs and lush forests frequently appear to conceal secrets.

Another favorite of mine is the Huldra, a forest spirit who entices men with her beauty but is supposed to have a hollow back and a cow's tail, indicating her supernatural nature. These stories demonstrate a strong reverence for nature, encouraging listeners to exercise caution in the woods.

Norwegian Customs
Norwegians commemorate folklore and traditions in distinct ways. For example, Christmas customs are influenced by ancient beliefs. The nisse, a little, mischievous gnome-like creature, is thought to safeguard crops if handled well. People leave him oatmeal with butter to ensure he brings good luck.

Another unique ritual is Midsummer Eve, sometimes known as St. Hans. It's a summer solstice festival with bonfires and community gatherings that incorporate both pagan and Christian elements.

Cultural Highlights
Bunads, which are traditional Norwegian costumes worn at events such as Norwegian Constitution Day (May 17th), were one of the best ways for me to experience Norwegian traditions. Each region has its distinct pattern, which features delicate needlework and craftsmanship passed down through generations.

Additionally, I thought the traditional music, particularly the haunting strains of the Hardanger fiddle, to be really affecting. This instrument, embellished with stunning graphics, generates a sound as captivating as the landscapes it depicts.

Modern Connections
Norwegian folklore lives on today, not only in stories but also in current culture. Films, novels, and even attractions such as the Trollstigen Road and Trolltunga pay homage to these fabled characters. At the same time, traditional events continue to bring people together by combining the past and the present.

As I researched this rich tradition, I discovered that Norwegian folklore is more than simply stories; it reflects the people's connection to their land, respect for nature, and love of storytelling. Every corner of Norway appeared to have a story ready to be told. If you're visiting this beautiful country, I highly recommend immersing yourself in its stories and traditions—they really bring the landscapes to life.

Historic Villages and Local Life

When I visit Norway, I am frequently drawn to its attractive ancient communities and vibrant local life. Norway's legacy is rich, with historic traditions and thriving rural villages dating back millennia. Each community I visit has its own unique tale, and there's something magical about roaming around locations with such a strong connection to their past.

I usually recommend Gudvangen, located in the center of the Naerøyfjord. This village feels like stepping back in time. It is surrounded by tall mountains, and historic wooden structures lend it a timeless atmosphere. Gudvangen also has a Viking village, where I've been able to participate in living history activities such as reenactments, historical crafts, and Viking feasts. It's an immersive way to learn about how early Norwegians lived, and I always leave with a great understanding of the region's history.

Another place that stands out to me is Lofoten, which is located above the Arctic Circle. The Lofoten Islands are recognized for their harsh beauty, which includes steep mountains rising from the sea. I've spent hours meandering through Reine, one of the most beautiful settlements, and the gorgeous red and yellow fisherman's cabins known as rorbu are impossible not to admire. These huts were originally used by fishermen, but they now provide a comfortable, authentic stay for visitors wishing to immerse themselves in local culture. I've had the pleasure of trying local fish dishes, particularly dried cod, which has been a mainstay in this region for decades.

In Røros, another heritage wonder, I felt like I was in a live museum. It's a mining village from the 17th century, and its well-preserved wooden buildings have won it UNESCO World Heritage designation. Walking along the cobbled streets, I felt a connection with the people who lived here, especially when I visited the historic Røros Church or stopped by local artisan workshops where crafts like wood carving are still practiced.

What impresses me the most about visiting these villages is the sense of pride in maintaining the past while welcoming the future. Locals in these historic villages take great care to preserve their traditions, including language, architecture, and culinary habits. It's evident that heritage sites like these are more than just tourist attractions; they're living, breathing symbols of Norwegian identity.

Exploring these communities is essential for anybody interested in learning more about Norway's cultural heritage. Whether appreciating the stunning splendor of Voss or having a quiet evening in Henningsvær, the country's rich heritage shapes local life and creates unique memories for visitors like me.

Museum Visits and Cultural Hotspots

Exploring the museums and cultural hotspots around Norway's fjords takes you through history, art, and the country's unique traditions. Allow me to share with you the most captivating spots I've seen, all of which are updated for the current season.

Bryggen Museum, Bergen

Entering Bergen's Bryggen Museum was like walking through time. This museum, built on the remains of medieval Bergen, displays items from the city's Hanseatic era. I was particularly drawn to the beautiful pottery and equipment that depict the daily lives of the merchants who formed this UNESCO World Heritage site. The museum's position near the historic Bryggen Wharf makes it both culturally and historically significant.

Norwegian Fisheries Museum

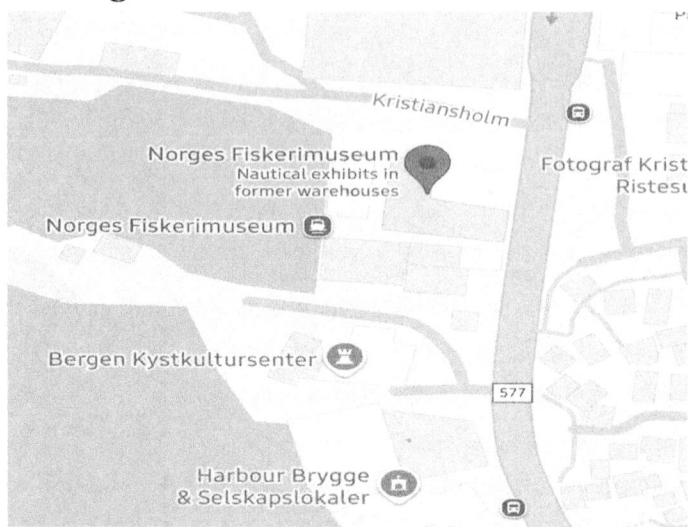

If you want to learn about Norway's deep relationship to the sea, this museum is a must-see. The Norwegian Fisheries Museum, located in Bergen, also provides hands-on exhibitions about the fishing industry, which has been crucial to the fjord regions for centuries. My favorite part was the interactive area, where I learnt about sustainable fishing practices and even practiced "casting a net" in a simulation.

Aalesunds Museum, Ålesund

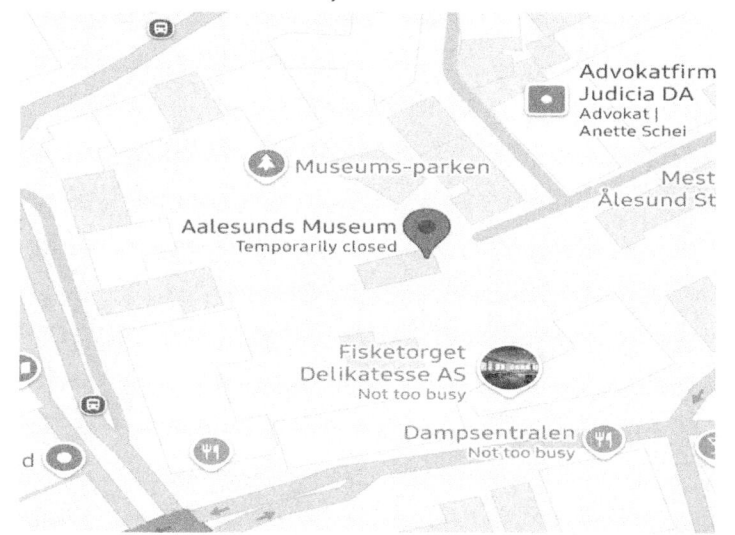

In the picturesque town of Alesund, I went to the Aalesunds Museum, a hidden gem that chronicles the town's rebuilding following the 1904 fire. The Art Nouveau architecture is magnificent, and the displays cover maritime history and local folklore. I ascended the adjacent Aksla Viewpoint for a fantastic vista. It was worth every step.

The Flam Railway Museum in Flam

This museum, located in the tiny village of Flam, was delightful. It is free to visit, and the exhibits explain the tale of one of the world's steepest railways, the Flam Railway. I marveled at the engineering behind this miracle while viewing historical images and artifacts. It's small yet educational, and the ideal place to stop before or after a train journey.

Viking Ship Museum in Oslo (Update: Under Renovation)

Although Oslo is not immediately on the fjord cruise itinerary, it is frequently included in longer Norwegian itineraries. While the Viking Ship Museum is being renovated (it will reopen as the Museum of the Viking Age in 2025), you can still visit temporary Viking exhibitions throughout the city. If you enjoy history as much as I do, I recommend keeping this in mind for future vacations.

Nidaros Cathedral and Archbishop's Palace in Trondheim

The beautiful Nidaros Cathedral, a Gothic masterpiece, is located in Trondheim, which is accessible via certain lengthier fjord cruises. The nearby Archbishop's Palace Museum houses medieval antiques, and I got the opportunity to view the Norwegian crown jewels. It is a profoundly spiritual and cultural experience.

Cultural Hotspots
Visit local sights like the Seven Sisters Waterfall in Geiranger or experience live music at Tromsø's Arctic Cathedral to fully immerse yourself in the culture, in addition to the amazing museums. These

places connect you not only to Norway's past, but also to its vibrant, living culture today.

Chapter 6: Practical Tips for Cruising the Fjords

Packing Tips for a Fjord Cruise

When preparing for a fjord cruise, you must be prepared for Norway's ever-changing weather and the wide range of activities available. Here's my guide based on what works best for me and the latest travel updates:

Layer Smartly for the Weather
The Norwegian fjords are known for their unpredictable weather, so layering is necessary. Even throughout the summer, temperatures can

swing from frigid mornings to surprisingly warm afternoons.

Base Layers: Begin with thermal or moisture-wicking base layers to keep yourself warm and dry. These are especially necessary if you're going in the spring or fall, when temperatures are colder.

Mid-Layers: Bring fleece or wool sweaters for warmth. They are lightweight and easy to layer.

Outer Layers: A waterproof and windproof jacket is essential. Fjords can be windy, and rain showers are typical, even in the summer.

Clothing for Activities
Whether you're hiking, kayaking, or admiring stunning deck views, here's what I'd pack:

Hiking Gear: Comfortable, waterproof hiking boots are essential for outings such as visiting Geirangerfjord or hiking to Preikestolen (Pulpit Rock). Pack quick-drying hiking pants and breathable socks to reduce discomfort.

Casual Wear: Bring comfortable, warm clothing for aboard activities or strolling around picturesque villages such as Flam or Alesund.

Formal Attire: Many cruise lines include formal dinner nights, so bring one or two smart outfits.

Swimsuits: Yes, even in Norway! Some ships include hot tubs or spas, and if you're feeling daring, you may attempt a cold-water dip.

Accessories & Essentials
The appropriate equipment may make or break your trip. Here is my go-to list.

- **Daypack:** Ideal for bringing water, food, and layers during shore excursions.

- **Waterproof Gear:** Gloves, hats, and scarves are essential on cold, wet days.

- **Binoculars:** You'll want to see waterfalls, wildlife, and distant peaks.

- **Reusable Water Bottle:** Stay hydrated sustainably with Norway's tap water, which is among the best in the world.

- **Power Adaptor:** Norway accepts Type C or F plugs, so carry an adaptor if necessary.

Weather-Specific Tips

Summer (June–August)
Days are warmer, but carry sunscreen and sunglasses for protection during long bright days. Evenings can be cool, so wear a light jacket.

Winter (November–March)
Bring warm clothes and snow boots. The Northern Lights and icy landscapes are best seen during this season.

Spring/Autumn (April-May, September-October)
Expect cool weather and occasional rain. Layering is particularly important during these seasons.

Staying Connected

Staying connected on a Norwegian Fjord cruise is considerably easier than you may expect, given to the superb connectivity alternatives accessible in Norway. I discovered that the mix of solid cell networks, public Wi-Fi, and onboard amenities made it simple to stay in touch with friends and family while also navigating my vacation.

Internet and Mobile Coverage
Norway has one of the world's greatest mobile networks, with high-speed 4G and expanding 5G coverage, even in remote fjord locations. Throughout the cruise, I utilized a local SIM card from carriers such as Telenor or Telia. These firms provide prepaid plans with substantial data packages, ideal for vacationers. I recommend getting a SIM card at the airport or in major cities like Bergen because it's a cheap way to stay connected.

Mobile signals can occasionally weaken while sailing through more remote fjords, but I found that service usually returned once I got closer to towns or big tourist destinations like Geiranger or Flam. To minimize additional expenditures, I activated an international roaming plan before leaving home or used Wi-Fi whenever possible.

Public Wi-Fi
Many cafes, restaurants, and public spaces in Norway offer free Wi-Fi, particularly in larger towns such as Bergen, Alesund, and Stavanger. While touring Bergen's Bryggen Wharf or sipping

coffee on the Flam Railway, I quickly connected to free networks to share my travel experiences. Keep in mind that certain places may require a little fee or a login to gain access.

Onboard Internet
Most cruise ships that sail through the fjords include onboard internet access. These can be pricey, but they are useful if you need to keep connected on your trip. I found the connection steady enough for simple operations like email checking and browsing, but streaming and video calls were hit or miss.

Many cruise lines provide public computers or internet cafes for guests who prefer to unplug and enjoy the view.

Tips For Staying Connected

Download Offline Maps
I utilized apps like Google Maps and Maps.me to navigate fjord towns without an internet connection.

Portable Wi-Fi Hotspots

Renting a pocket Wi-Fi gadget is ideal for groups or families. These gadgets offer a private connection for several devices.

Cruise Applications

Many cruise lines now offer applications that allow guests to access daily schedules, activities, and messaging services through the ship's intranet, eliminating the need for external internet.

Health and Safety on Board and Off

When it comes to staying healthy and safe on your Norwegian Fjord cruise, there are a few key things to remember both on board and during excursions. Here are some pointers to help you have a comfortable and pleasurable journey.

Health and Safety Onboard

Today, cruise ships prioritize guest health by providing access to well-equipped medical facilities and health services whenever necessary. It's critical to stay hydrated, especially if you're in the north, where the air can be rather dry even in summer. To avoid windburn, drink plenty of water, wear sunscreen, and apply lip balm.

If you are prone to seasickness, it is a good idea to take precautions. Modern ships are extremely stable, however if you're prone to motion sickness, consider:

Medication
Over-the-counter medications such as Dramamine and natural therapies like ginger can assist.

Acupressure
Wristbands that apply pressure to the appropriate acupressure sites can help reduce nausea.

Location
If you're feeling uneasy, head to the center of the ship, where there's less motion.

It is also critical to adhere to onboard hygiene protocols, particularly during flu season or if COVID-19 is still an issue. Washing your hands on a regular basis and using hand sanitizers that are accessible in public places will help you stay healthy.

Health and Safety on Excursions
When leaving the ship for excursions, it is critical to keep safety in mind, especially during vigorous

sports such as hiking, kayaking, or bicycling. Here are some tips:

Proper Gear
Always wear comfortable hiking or walking shoes. If you intend to visit tough terrain, ensure your footwear is durable. Layer your clothing to adjust to changing weather conditions, and always include a rain jacket because the weather in Norway may be unpredictable.

Safety Briefings
Pay close attention to any safety briefings provided prior to trips. Local guides are available to assist you stay safe, but it is your responsibility to heed their recommendations, especially when it comes to animal or water-based activities.

Physical Preparation
If you're going on a physically demanding expedition, such as a hike or a bike tour, be sure you're physically ready. Take it slowly and hydrate frequently. If you are unsure about your physical ability, choose easier, more relaxed activities to assure your comfort.

Emergency Situations and Medical Assistance

In the event of an emergency, cruise ships have well-equipped medical facilities, and most excursions include insurance for minor injuries. However, if you have any pre-existing medical concerns, you should consult your cruise line's medical team or pack any essential medications.

During excursions, always keep the ship's emergency contact information and a small first-aid kit on hand, especially if you're going to remote areas. Consider getting travel insurance that covers medical emergencies, especially if you're going on an adventurous trip like kayaking or trekking at high elevations.

Chapter 7: Transportation in the Norwegian Fjords

Getting to the Norwegian Fjords

When planning a journey to the stunning Norwegian Fjords, there are various ways to get there, whether by air, rail, or water. Allow me to lead you through the most popular and convenient ways to visit these breathtaking natural treasures.

Flights
One of the quickest and most usual methods to reach the Norwegian Fjords is to fly into one of

Norway's main airports. The most commonly used entry points are:

Oslo Airport (Gardermoen)
As the capital's primary international gateway, Oslo Gardermoen has excellent connections to a variety of global locations. Domestic flights from Oslo connect to smaller airports in the fjords, including Bergen, Tromsø, and Alesund.

Bergen Airport (Flesland)
Bergen is frequently regarded as the gateway to the fjords, and Bergen Airport provides direct flights from locations around Europe, particularly during the summer. Once you arrive in Bergen, you'll be close to breathtaking fjords such as Hardangerfjord and Sognefjord.

Tromsø Airport
For those interested in the Arctic regions of the fjords, Tromsø offers a more northerly option, with access to fjords in northern Norway, including Lyngenfjord and Kongsfjorden. Tromsø is a great place to watch the Northern Lights during the winter months.

Train Travel

If you want a more leisurely and scenic journey to the fjords, consider taking the train. Norway's train network is well-maintained, and some routes are particularly noted for their breathtaking views:

Oslo to Bergen
The Oslo-Bergen railway is often regarded as one of the most scenic train rides in the world. Before arriving in Bergen, you will see Norway's breathtaking scenery as you journey through mountains, woods, and valleys. The trek takes about 7 hours and is a nice opportunity to explore the country's natural beauty.

Flåm Railway
Located in the fjord region, the Flåm Railway connects Flam to Myrdal via one of the world's steepest railway tracks. This journey takes you over magnificent mountains with breathtaking views of the Aurlandsfjord.

Ferries and Cruise Ships
The greatest way to visit Norway's fjords is by water, and happily, there are various options:

Ferries
Ferries are a popular and practical way to reach the fjords. Many ferry routes connect coastal

communities and fjord regions. Ferries travel from Bergen to Flåm and Alesund to Geirangerfjord. These routes offer not only transportation but also the opportunity to experience the beautiful grandeur of the fjords from the water.

Cruise Ships
Norway is well-known for its fjord cruises, with many major cruise companies operating in the area. Cruises often sail from places such as Bergen, Oslo, and Alesund and provide multi-day excursions to the most famous fjords. Popular cruises include Hurtigruten, which sails along Norway's coast, as well as fjord cruises to sites such as Geirangerfjord, Sognefjord, and Hardangerfjord.

Getting Around The Fjords

When traveling through the Norwegian Fjords, you need to know how to navigate around after you get to your location. While the fjords themselves provide stunning views, getting between them and the surrounding areas takes some forethought. Here's an overview of the local transportation choices you might anticipate to use throughout your fjord excursion.

Buses

The bus is one of the most convenient ways to travel around the fjords. Many of the major fjord towns, including Bergen, Flam, Alesund, and Geiranger, are connected by public transport. These buses are generally reliable, with routes designed to accommodate both locals and visitors. In addition to ordinary public buses, sightseeing buses are offered in several areas, particularly major tourist destinations such as Flam and Geiranger. These trips frequently feature guided commentary, making them an excellent way to learn about the history and culture of the fjords while admiring the scenery.

Ferries and Water Taxi
Because many of the fjords are surrounded by steep mountains and secluded islands, ferries and water taxis are necessary routes of transit. Ferries are a popular and economical means to travel between fjords, such as Bergen to Flam or Alesund to Geiranger. Some of these ferry routes also provide fantastic sightseeing possibilities, allowing you to experience the fjords from a new angle. Water taxis offer a more personal and flexible way to explore tiny islands or more remote places. They are frequently available on demand and can transport you to locations not easily accessible by other means.

Car Rentals

Renting a car is another alternative, especially if you want to explore the fjords at your own time. Car rentals are accessible in most major cities, including Bergen and Alesund, allowing you to reach isolated, off-the-beaten-path spots. Some regions, such as the Sognefjord and Hardangerfjord, are ideal for scenic drives, and having a car allows you to visit smaller communities, hiking trails, and overlooks along the way. However, driving in the fjords might be challenging. Many roads are narrow and twisting, especially in more rocky locations, and parking may be scarce in smaller towns. Furthermore, some of the more popular fjords, such as Geirangerfjord, may have limited car access during busy seasons, so plan ahead.

Cruise Ports and Shore Excursions

When I went on my Norwegian Fjord cruise, I was excited to discover the distinct charms of each port we visited. From Alesund to Flam to Tromsø, each site had its own allure, along with numerous transportation options and shore activities that made the journey memorable. Here's my guide to the ports, their transit options, and the excursions you should not miss.

Alesund

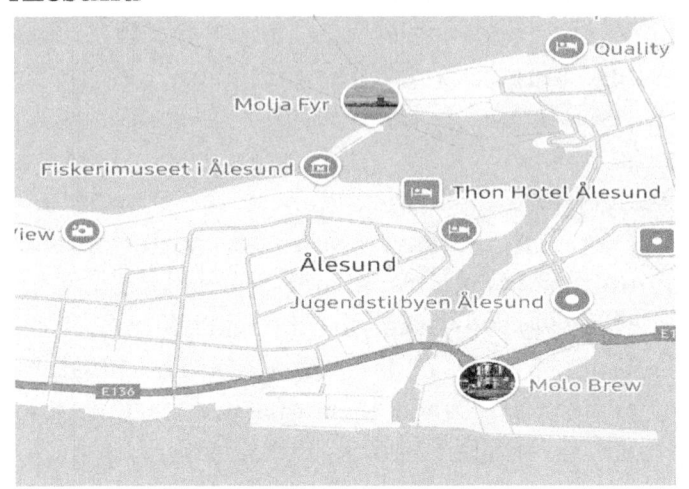

Alesund, famed for its Art Nouveau design, is a harbor that combines modern amenities with historic charm. When you exit from your cruise, you will find that the dock is only a short walk from the city center. If you want to travel further, cabs and shuttle buses are readily available, and there is also a local bus network if you prefer public transportation.

Alesund provides a range of shore trip possibilities. I definitely recommend the Aksla Viewpoint walk, which provides breathtaking views of the city and neighboring islands. For a more leisurely experience, take a boat tour of the local islands or visit the Atlantic Sea Park, Northern Europe's largest saltwater aquarium. If you enjoy history, the Art Nouveau Center is a must-see.

Flam

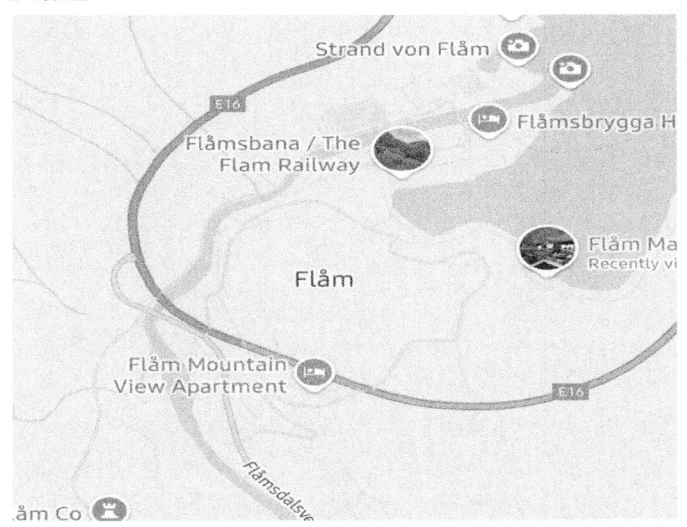

Flam, located at the end of the Aurlandsfjord, is one of the most magnificent ports you will see. The harbor is relatively accessible, and there is a small transportation hub that connects you to Flam's main attractions. The Flam Railway provided an excellent experience for me. It's regarded as one of the most picturesque train trips in the world, passing through steep hillsides and past gushing waterfalls.

Taxis are available for those interested in exploring further, but I recommend arranging a fjord cruise. Sailing on the Naerøyfjord, a UNESCO World Heritage site, provides access to breathtaking scenery. For hikers, there are numerous paths with fjord views, including a difficult but rewarding climb up Mount Rjoandefossen.

Tromsø

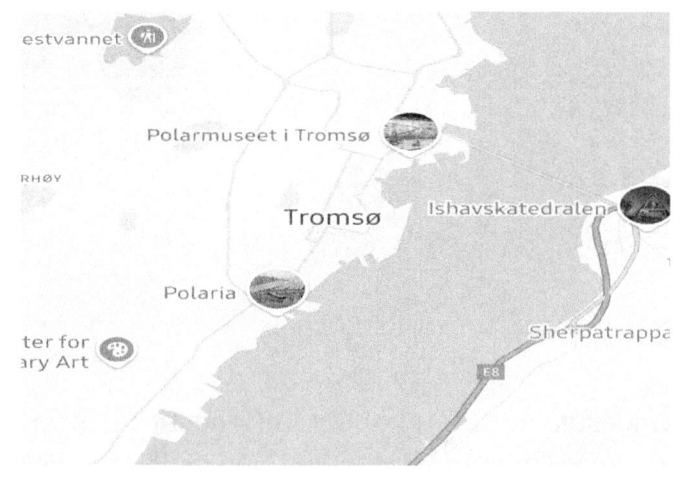

As you go north, Tromsø provides a unique Arctic experience. The port is well-connected, with taxis, shuttle buses, and even public transportation to get you into the heart of the city. to learn about Tromsø's role in Arctic exploration, visit the Polar Museum. Alternatively, take the Fjellheisen Cable Car up Mount Storsteinen for breathtaking views of the city and surrounding landscapes.

One of the delights of Tromsø is the opportunity to witness the Northern Lights. There are several trips offered that will take you to great spots for Aurora watching. You can also take a whale-watching excursion (during the winter) or go dog-sledding to see Arctic wildlife.

General Shore Excursion Tips
Regardless of your port, I recommend reserving shore excursions in advance, especially for popular attractions such as the Flam Railway or Northern Lights trips. Many excursions fill up quickly, so booking in advance might help you avoid disappointment. Furthermore, local guides are provided at most ports, allowing you to immerse yourself in the culture and history of each destination.

Eco-Friendly Transportation

When I visited the Norwegian Fjords, one of my top concerns was to explore this beautiful landscape in an environmentally sustainable manner. Sustainability is strongly established in the Norwegian way of life, and there are numerous ways to travel responsibly while enjoying the splendor of the fjords.

Electric Vehicles
Renting an electric vehicle (EV) is an excellent option for getting around the fjord regions. Norway leads in EV adoption, with substantial charging infrastructure even in remote locations. I was astounded by how easy it was to find a charging station along major roads such as the Norwegian Scenic roads, which offer stunning views while encouraging low-emission travel. Many rental firms in Norway now offer electric vehicles, making it easy for holidaymakers to lessen their carbon footprint.

Cycling
Cycling provides a more immersive experience. The fjord region is bike-friendly, with designated bike paths and routes such as the Rallarvegen, which is regarded as one of Norway's most scenic cycling routes. It's more than just lowering emissions; it's also about fully connecting with the peaceful landscapes. E-bikes were especially useful for conquering steep inclines, making the journey more fun while requiring less work.

Public Transportation
Norway's public transportation system is both environmentally sustainable and convenient. Buses,

ferries, and trains are all great ways to travel around, with many of them powered by renewable energy. The Flam Railway, for example, provides a wonderful tour across the fjords while focusing on sustainability. Similarly, I found ferries like the electric Vision of the Fjords to be a guilt-free way to enjoy the rivers while reducing pollution.

Traveling responsibly across the Norwegian Fjords is more than just about conserving the environment; it's also about appreciating the beauty of these natural treasures. By selecting green options such as EVs, bicycles, and public transportation, you can ensure your vacation leaves the fjords as pristine as you found them.

Chapter 8: Shopping, Dining, and Souvenirs

Best Souvenirs from the Fjords

When I visited the Norwegian Fjords, I learned that the finest mementos are not only gorgeous but also have a strong connection to Norway's rich cultural past. Here are some of my top recommendations:

Local Handicrafts
One of the most memorable souvenirs you may bring home from the fjords is a handcrafted item created by local craftspeople. Norway is known for its wood carvings, troll sculptures, and

hand-painted pottery. These one-of-a-kind creations represent the country's long-standing handicraft traditions and frequently incorporate elements from nature, folklore, and Viking history. I discovered numerous wonderful shops in the fjord towns that sold similar goods, which were often handcrafted from locally sourced materials.

Woolen Goods
Norwegian wool is well-known for its warmth and durability, making it ideal for the cold weather in the fjords. I was astounded by the range of woolen sweaters (including the legendary Lusekofte), scarves, caps, and mittens available for purchase. The Setesdal sweater, with its beautiful patterns, is a distinctive item that I strongly suggest. These knitted goods are not only functional, but also make lovely, fashionable gifts to carry home.

Norwegian Culinary Items
I wanted to bring Norwegian cuisine culture home with me, and I am pleased I did! These culinary delicacies, ranging from brown cheese (Brunost), a sweet and delicious delight, to dried meats such as jerky, provide a unique way to remember the fjords. I also discovered Norwegian jam produced with native berries such as lingonberries and cloudberries, which would make an excellent

complement to breakfast at home. For those who enjoy cooking, I propose reintroducing some traditional Norwegian spices and baking ingredients to help reproduce the flavors of Norway in your own kitchen.

These gifts not only serve as physical reminders of my vacation, but they also connect me to the customs and local life of the fjord settlements. Whether you're looking for a warm woolen sweater, a handcrafted item, or a delectable Norwegian delicacy, these souvenirs are ideal keepsakes to remind you of your amazing trip to the Fjords.

Top Restaurants & Local Dining Experiences

When embarking on a Norwegian Fjord cruise, one of the joys is sampling the local cuisine. Whether you're in Bergen, Flam, Alesund, or Geiranger, there are various places to eat real Norwegian cuisine that reflects the country's rich culture and beautiful landscape. Here's where I propose eating and what you should try:

Bergen

Bergen is well-known for its fresh seafood, thanks to its proximity to the ocean. You should definitely go to Bryggen's Fish Market, a bustling market where you may sample fresh catches of the day. Try klippfisk (dried and salted cod) or the famous Norwegian crab. For a classy eating experience, I heartily recommend Enhjørningen in Bryggen. This restaurant specializes in traditional Norwegian cuisine, such as raspeballer (potato dumplings) and reinsdyr (reindeer), which are served with a fine Norwegian wine. Don't miss their Koldtbord, a Scandinavian cold buffet featuring a variety of meats, cheeses, and breads.

Flam

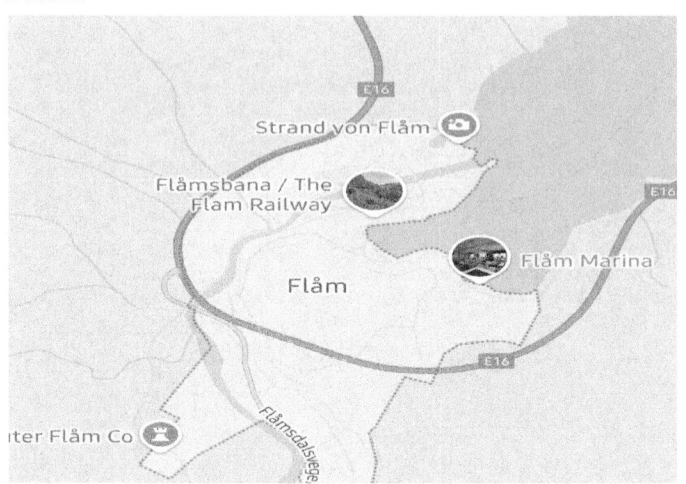

Flam, located in the center of Sognefjord, provides dining experiences that allow you to appreciate the magnificent fjord views while sampling local flavors. Flam Marina and Apartments offers a comfortable atmosphere and cuisine like laks (salmon), a Norwegian classic. For a warm drink, visit Ægir BrewPub, which offers artisan brews and a Viking-inspired menu, including local lamb and root vegetable stew. The beer and food combos here are popular with everyone eager to try something new.

Alesund

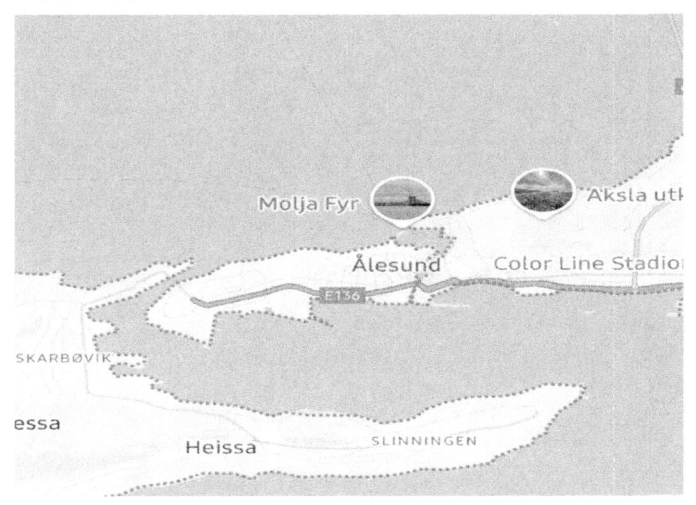

Alesund is known for its Art Nouveau architecture and seafood. One must-try restaurant is Sjøbua, located by the water. Local delicacies include fish soup and skrei (cod), but it's the lobster dishes that steal the show. For a more upmarket experience, Fjord restaurant serves a modern take on traditional Norwegian dishes with a spectacular view of the fjord. Their mussels and reindeer steak are popular, and they frequently employ products sourced directly from the nearby mountains and rivers.

Geiranger

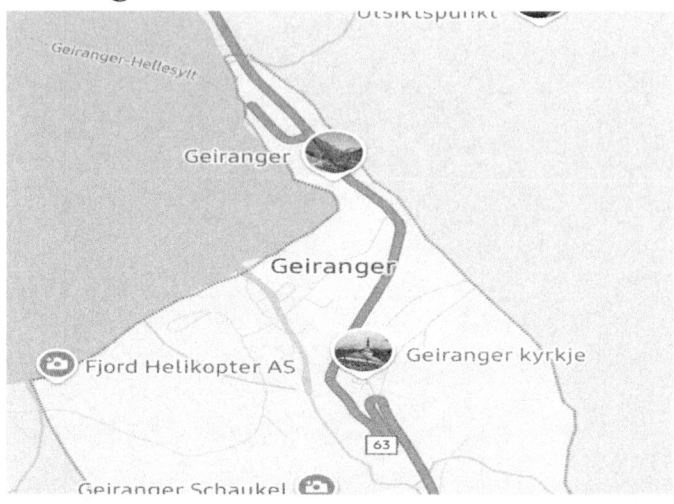

Geiranger is a tranquil community surrounded by stunning waterfalls and rocks. I recommend Brasserie Posten, which serves both classic Norwegian cooking and more contemporary meals. The venison stew and local fish are fantastic options. Geiranger Bakeri, a more relaxed option, serves fresh pastries and coffee while overlooking the fjord.

What to Try?

Lutefisk
Dried fish rehydrated in a lye solution, typically eaten with potatoes, peas, and bacon. It's a

traditional Norwegian meal that can be found at numerous restaurants along the fjords.

Rømmegrøt
Is a creamy porridge made with sour cream, butter, sugar, and cinnamon. Locals adore this soothing dish, which is typically served with cured meats.

Kjøttkaker
Norwegian meatballs cooked from ground beef and pork, typically eaten with potatoes and brown gravy.

Wherever you are in the Norwegian Fjords, you will enjoy excellent, regionally inspired foods that will make your cruise experience even more unforgettable!

Shopping at Norwegian Fjord Ports

When cruising through the breathtaking Norwegian Fjords, one of the joys is frequently the opportunity to shop in quaint cities such as Bergen and Alesund. Both are ideal for purchasing one-of-a-kind souvenirs, high-quality Norwegian handicrafts, and presents that reflect the region's natural beauty and culture.

Shop in Bergen
Bergen, with its scenic waterfront and historic charm, offers a wide range of retail options. Bryggen Wharf is a must-see. This UNESCO World Heritage site is surrounded by vibrant wooden houses that host artisan businesses selling anything from handcrafted jewelry to local artwork. Shops provide Norwegian wool products, such as plush wool sweaters and scarves.

Torgallmenningen, the city's major retail street, is a must-see for anyone who enjoys high-end goods and international shopping. It is surrounded with fashion boutiques, bookstores, and department stores, making it the ideal location for finding everything from trendy clothing to unusual presents. Don't miss the Fish Market, where you can pick up local delicacies like dried fish and Norwegian chocolate to take home as wonderful mementos.

Shop in Alesund
Alesund, famed for its Art Nouveau buildings, offers a unique shopping experience. In the town center, there are several boutiques and galleries selling unique Norwegian products including trolls, Lofoten ceramics, and Sami jewelry. Alesund's bustling environment is reflected in its local stores,

which specialize in high-quality products created by local artists.

For those interested in learning more about Norwegian heritage, visit Kremmer Garden, a well-known retail complex in Alesund that sells a wide range of Norwegian-designed products, including home decor and clothing. You may also shop at Alesund's Art Nouveau Centre for gorgeous prints and artwork inspired by the town's famous architectural style.

Tips for Shopping at Norwegian Fjord Ports

Currency
Norway utilizes the Norwegian krone (NOK), so make sure you exchange money or use credit cards that do not impose international transaction fees. Many shops accept Euros, however it's always a good idea to double-check.

Opening Hours
Shops in Norwegian Fjord communities are typically open from 9:00 a.m. to 6:00 p.m., with extended hours on Saturdays. Some may close sooner on Sundays.

Unique Finds

Norwegian designs are noted for their simplicity and superb quality. Wool clothes, woodwork handicrafts, and locally produced food items such as cheese and jam make excellent souvenirs.

Shopping in the Norwegian Fjord ports, such as Bergen and Alesund, is an experience in and of itself, allowing you to take a bit of Norway home.

Chapter 9: Itinerary for Norwegian Fjord Cruise

Day 1: Bergen

Morning: Arrival in Bergen
My journey begins in Bergen, a picturesque city set between mountains and fjords. As soon as I arrive, I go straight to Bryggen, a UNESCO World Heritage Site. The old wooden structures here date from the 14th century, and the neighborhood has been scrupulously restored to maintain its true medieval atmosphere. I stroll down the cobblestone streets, admiring the colorful stores, museums, and art galleries that line the shore. After that, I visit the

Fish Market, a bustling hub that sells fresh seafood, local veggies, and Norwegian specialties. It's the ideal place to grab a quick bite or simply enjoy the lively ambiance.

Afternoon: Ride the Fløibanen Funicular
In the afternoon, I head to the Fløibanen Funicular. The iconic funicular journey to Mount Fløyen offers stunning views of Bergen, the port, and neighboring fjords. From the summit, I can see the city snuggled among beautiful green hills, and the big sea in the distance. It's a chance to soak it all in, and if I'm feeling brave, I can tackle one of the many hiking paths that round the hilltop. Whether I want to explore further or simply rest with a coffee at the top, it's an excellent way to get a feel for the city from above.

Evening: Dinner at Enhjørningen
As the sun sets, I head to Enhjørningen, one of Bergen's finest fish restaurants. Located in a historic wooden building near the waterfront, this restaurant serves some of the city's freshest fish. I adore Norwegian specialties such as klippfisk (dried and salted fish) and seafood platters. The environment is cozy and welcoming, giving it the perfect place to reflect on my first day in this lovely city. After a lovely supper, I take a leisurely stroll

along the harbor, soaking up the peaceful evening atmosphere before returning to my lodging for the night.

Day 2: Stavanger

Morning: Arrive in Stavanger

I arrived in Stavanger early in the morning, eager to see one of Norway's most iconic sites. I couldn't wait to see Preikestolen, popularly known as Pulpit Rock. It is one of the world's most photographed natural wonders, rising 604 meters above the Lysefjord. The hike to Pulpit Rock is a must-do excursion, with stunning views of the surrounding fjord. It's a moderate trek that takes around 4-5 hours round trip, but every step is worthwhile because of the breathtaking panoramic vistas at the top. If you're not up for the climb, there are guided trips that will take you directly to the base of the rock, where you can still enjoy the scenery. The crystal-clear ocean below and the high cliffs provide a breathtaking spectacle, especially on a clear day.

Afternoon: Exploring Stavanger
Following the hike, I returned to Stavanger to explore the city itself. The Old Town of Stavanger, also known as Gamle Stavanger, is attractive with its cobblestone lanes and 18th-century intact wooden homes. It's a beautiful spot to walk about and soak up the ambiance.

I also visited the Norwegian Petroleum Museum, which provides an interesting look at Norway's oil history and its impact on the country's development. Stavanger has gained the nickname "Oil Capital" of Norway, and the museum explains how the oil business has impacted the city and the country. If you want to learn more about Norway's economic growth, this museum is a must-see.

Evening: Dinner in Stavanger
As the evening progressed, I chose between relaxing on board for a leisurely meal and exploring Stavanger's culinary scene. The city is known for its fresh seafood, so I couldn't pass up eating some of the local specialties. Fisketorget, or the Fish

Market, is an excellent place to enjoy fish near the waterfront. I had the Reker (Norwegian shrimp), which was incredibly fresh. If you're looking for something more modern, Stavanger features a number of fashionable restaurants that serve Nordic cuisine, ranging from fine dining to casual locations. I ended up having dinner onboard, admiring the gorgeous sights from the ship and thinking about the day's activities.

Day 3: Geirangerfjord

Morning
Today, I woke up to the promise of one of Norway's most iconic and beautiful fjords: Geirangerfjord. The ship glides through the narrow, peaceful seas, surrounded by towering cliffs and rich foliage. As

we approach, I feel as if I've entered a fantastic universe, surrounded by the fjord's stunning splendor. Geirangerfjord is known for its breathtaking natural beauty, with crystal-clear waters mirroring the steep mountain slopes. As we float around the fjord, I can't help but be impressed by its magnificence, which has won it the UNESCO World Heritage classification. This morning's sail is an excellent introduction to the splendor that awaits me.

Afternoon
After the cruise, it's time for some adventure. I decided to trek to Dalsnibba, a peak with stunning panoramic views of the fjord. The trek is difficult, but the payoff is well worth it—the view from the summit is breathtaking, with the fjord sprawling out underneath me in all its magnificence. If I'm not up for the climb, I can take a boat trip of the fjord to go near the famous Seven Sisters Waterfall. The waterfalls are as breathtaking as they sound, with water flowing down the cliff walls in several streams, creating a sight right out of a storybook.

Evening
As the day comes to a close, I have a nice meal onboard while seeing the breathtaking fjord landscape fade away behind us. The mix of superb

meals and the grandeur of the fjord creates an amazing experience. From my seat, I can still see the delicate gleam of sunshine on the river and the distant mountains' silhouettes. It's the ideal approach to reflect on the day's adventures while admiring the beauty of Geirangerfjord.

Day 4: Alesund

Morning
I arrived in Alesund, a lovely town known for its unique Art Nouveau architecture. The town's distinct appearance is the product of a devastating fire in 1904, which forced a complete rebuild in this architectural style. As I go through the streets, I am immediately drawn to the elaborate façade, decorative embellishments, and bright buildings

that flank the town. It's more than just a location to visit; it's like stepping into a live artwork. I definitely recommend meandering through the Alesund Town Center, which has not just old buildings but also a variety of attractive shops, cafes, and galleries.

Afternoon

After taking in the town's charm, I make the short but spectacular climb up to Aksla Viewpoint, which is a must-see for anybody visiting Alesund. From my vantage point, I get an incredible panoramic view of the town, the Archipelago, and the neighboring fjords. The vista is breathtaking: rolling hills, glittering waters, and clusters of islands, all sprinkled with colorful dwellings below. I can even see the nearby mountains and the picturesque seashore. It's one of those views that is so stunning that it nearly seems surreal. The viewpoint is accessible via a tiny, well-kept walk, or I can take the bus for a more leisurely ride up.

Evening

As the evening draws in, I have two excellent eating alternatives to pick from. To experience the local ambiance, visit Sjøbua, a seafood restaurant that serves fresh fish and mackerel. The restaurant's pleasant setting makes it the ideal place to unwind and reflect on the day's events. Alternatively, I can spend a relaxing evening on the cruise, where I'll be treated to a fantastic meal while admiring the peaceful nighttime vistas of the fjords as we sail toward our next destination.

Day 5: Flam and Sognefjord

Morning: Arrive at Flam

I awoke to the crisp, fresh air of Flam, situated in the middle of the Sognefjord. After a substantial breakfast on board, I set out for a ride on the famous Flam Railway. This train ride is truly amazing, going through beautiful green valleys and passing cascading waterfalls. As we went higher, the scenery got more striking, with towering mountains, peaceful fjords, and beautiful settlements dotting the landscape. It's widely referred to as one of the most picturesque train trips in the world, and I can see why. It was an excellent introduction to the natural splendor of this region, and a reminder of how much pristine beauty there is to find in Norway.

Afternoon: Cruise through the Sognefjord
After returning to Flam, I boarded the boat for the Sognefjord trip, excited to explore one of the world's longest and deepest fjords. The river was incredibly motionless, reflecting the towering cliffs and rich flora on each side. The backdrop was breathtaking, with towering mountains, peaceful waterways, and small farms dotting the fjord's beaches. It seemed like stepping into a postcard, and as we cruised farther into the fjord, I couldn't help but feel awestruck. This section of the fjord system is home to numerous small communities and lonely farms that can only be reached by boat or on foot, contributing to the sense of isolation and tranquillity.

Evening: Dinner and Relaxation Onboard
By the time we returned to the ship, I was ready to unwind and reflect on the day's activities. Dinner on board was an excellent opportunity to unwind and share experiences with fellow tourists. There's

something about cruising's leisurely, steady pace that allows you to completely enjoy the beauty around you, and tonight, I savored every morsel of Norwegian specialties, knowing that tomorrow's travels will be equally stunning. The social atmosphere was friendly and welcoming, allowing me to connect with individuals who shared my admiration for the stunning fjords we had seen.

Day 6: Tromsø

Morning
After a calm night at sea, we arrive in Tromsø, sometimes known as the "Gateway to the Arctic." The air is crisp and the landscape is spectacular. Tromsø is a picturesque town with rich history and culture. I start by visiting the Arctic-Alpine Botanic Garden, which is one of the world's northernmost

botanical gardens. Here, I have a unique opportunity to view Arctic and Alpine flora in bloom, demonstrating the persistence of life in this hard yet beautiful environment.

Alternatively, I visit Polaria, a beautiful Arctic center that houses exhibits on Arctic wildlife, the environment, and the intriguing phenomenon of the Northern Lights. The live displays of Arctic sea life and the panoramic movie provide a sense of the polar area. Tromsø has a lively cultural scene, so if I have time, I'll explore the local stores and galleries to experience the Arctic charm.

Afternoon
Now that I've experienced some culture and environment, it's time for a nice local meal. Tromsø is known for its Arctic food, and I recommend trying reindeer, a local specialty. The soft meat is frequently served with a rich sauce and mashed root vegetables or lingonberries, creating a lovely flavor combination that reflects the harsh beauty of the country.

Visiting Tromsø during the winter months is a great opportunity to see the Northern Lights. I decided to take an afternoon trip to visit this natural gem. Tromsø's location within the Aurora Belt increases the likelihood of seeing the lights, creating a breathtaking experience as they dance across the Arctic sky. During this time of year, the sun does not rise too high above the horizon, adding to the mystical quality of the encounter.

Evening

After a thrilling day of exploration, I return to the ship for supper. As I unwind, I ponder on the magnificent views I've seen today. During my Norwegian Fjord cruise, Tromsø was one of the most memorable stops due to its Arctic beauty, cultural history, and culinary delights. I eat my dinner onboard as the ship sets sail, eagerly anticipating tomorrow's excursions.

Day 7: Return to Bergen

Morning

As the cruise ship heads back to Bergen, I can't help but feel a mix of excitement and ease. The morning on deck is an ideal time to decompress. I take in the fresh air and breathtaking coastline surroundings, possibly enjoying a coffee or participating in one of the onboard activities to make the most of my final day at sea. Whether it's a cooking demonstration, a spa treatment, or simply sitting with a good book, it's a terrific way to spend the last few hours before heading into the city.

Afternoon

The ferry slowly approaches Bergen, and the panoramic views of the coast are truly beautiful. I can see the high mountains in the distance, as well as the gorgeous coastline with tiny settlements dotting the landscape. As we approach the city, I spend the afternoon staring out from the deck, taking in the natural beauty of the Norwegian coast for the last time. The tranquil atmosphere is ideal for reflecting on the great experiences I had on the cruise.

Evening
By dark, the ship had moored in Bergen, and it was time to depart. If my flight or travel plans allow, I may choose to spend a few additional hours touring Bergen before departing. There's always something new to explore, from the colorful structures of Bryggen to the brilliant street art that can be found around the city. I may also stop by a local café for a final taste of Norwegian cuisine, such as a hearty bowl of fish soup or fresh seafood. For those with limited time, a leisurely stroll around the port and a quick stop at a couple of the local stores could be the ideal way to end the journey.

Conclusion

As I think of the amazing beauty of the Norwegian Fjords, I can't help but be inspired by the spectacular scenery, tranquil waterways, and distinct culture of this incredible region of the world. Whether you're cruising through the small fjords of Geirangerfjord, exploring the charming village of Alesund, or admiring the boundless views from the summit of Dalsnibba, every minute in Norway makes you feel more connected to nature.

This tour is more than just seeing the views; it's about appreciating the slower pace of life that a fjord cruise provides. The tranquility of the lake, the fresh air, and the sensation of amazement from the towering cliffs and lush green hills are memories that will last long after the vacation is over.

I encourage you to take the plunge and go on your own Norwegian Fjord cruise. Whether you have a few days or a week, there is so much to learn. Plan your trip around your interests, whether it's seeing lovely villages, trekking to spectacular views, or simply resting onboard as you sail through some of the world's most gorgeous waters. Don't forget to bring your camera; these are memories you'll want to save.

As you explore the fjords, keep in mind that this is only the beginning. Norway offers more than just fjords, with lively towns like Oslo and Bergen, as well as Arctic treasures in Tromsø and the Lofoten Islands. This cruise is an excellent way to get a taste of Scandinavia's beauty and peacefulness, but there is so much more to see.

So, consider this book an invitation to begin planning, and remember that every day spent exploring the Norwegian Fjords is filled with awe, discovery, and amazing experiences. Begin your journey with an open heart, and let the fjords inspire you for your next adventure.

Printed in Great Britain
by Amazon